D0445978

The Business Wisdom of
STEVE JOBS

The Business Wisdom of
STEVE JOBS

250 QUOTES FROM THE INNOVATOR WHO CHANGED THE WORLD

Edited by Alan Ken Thomas

Skyhorse Publishing

Skyhorse Publishing books may be purchased in bulk at special discounts for sales promotion, corporate gifts, fund-raising, or educational purposes. Special editions can also be created to specifications. For details, contact the Special Sales Department, Skyhorse Publishing, 307 West 36th Street, 11th Floor, New York, NY 10018 or info@skyhorsepublishing.com.

Skyhorse® and Skyhorse Publishing® are registered trademarks of Skyhorse Publishing, Inc.®, a Delaware corporation.

www.skyhorsepublishing.com

10 9 8 7 6 5 4 3 2 1

Library of Congress Cataloging-in-Publication Data is available on file.
ISBN: 978-1-61608-749-4

Printed in the United States of America

Introduction

Even in death, people remain divided over Steve Jobs, the co-founder of Apple Inc. and known to the world as the man behind the iMac, iPod, iPhone, and iPad.

To some, Jobs was a man who changed the world for the better, an inventor and entrepreneur whose impact on daily life is immeasurable. To others, Jobs was a false idol, the symbol of everything wrong with a business playing its cards close to the vest. Everyone had an opinion about him.

But he wasn't always the center of attention. Steven Paul Jobs, born in San Francisco in 1955 and adopted and raised by Paul and Clara Jobs, was in fact a college dropout who found his lack of higher education hindering his path into the technology business. He eventually found work at burgeoning videogame company Atari, Inc., and it was around this time that he met Steve Wozniak.

It was a small, humble beginning: Jobs, Wozniak, and third partner Ronald Wayne founded Apple in 1976. A year later the "Apple II" was released to some success, but it wasn't until 1984, with a Superbowl ad and the release of the "Macintosh" that Apple really began the first of two creative and financial ascensions.

By all accounts, Jobs was a brilliant but difficult creative thinker, someone motivated by the idea that the simpler the design and the easier to use, the better the product. But his unorthodox ideas and ambitions eventually forced his resignation from Apple amidst power grabs by the company's board of directors and executives.

He left in 1985, and given the full history of the company, it's telling that in his absence Apple began to stagnate in innovation and products, while Jobs' two new ventures became the foundation for the later years of his life.

In the case of Pixar, originally a small graphic design offshoot of Lucasfilm, Jobs bought a $10 million company and sold it less than twenty years later for $7.4 billion to Disney. Along the way, the company revolutionized animation, starting with *Toy Story* and releasing successful full-length features almost every year since.

At NeXT Computer, Jobs' vision for the computer as an educational tool would eventually prove to be too cost-prohibitive for mass success, but the technical strengths of its hardware and software were years ahead of its time, something that even Apple recognized, acquiring the company in 1997 and bringing Jobs back with it.

And so began the history that pretty much everyone knows by now: first came the iMac, with its unique one-piece design and Technicolor hues. Then it was the iPod, turning the music industry on its head and marking the new age and format of digital music sales. The iPhone and iPad, elaborating on the iPod's idea of portability and accessibility, exceeded all expectations, solidifying Jobs' legacy and the second coming of Apple Inc., something not many people ever anticipated.

This book was written and researched on an iMac, with text messages from an iPhone vibrating on the table next to me, my girlfriend tapping on an iPad in the living room, and an iPod updating on iTunes in the computer's background. Typing out that sentence and re-reading it struck me as odd—it made me seem like a fanboy obsessed with the "cult of Mac." But then two things hit me: one, that an extraordinary amount of my day is built around products Steve Jobs oversaw the making of, and two, that my current situation is not one confined to a select few technophiles.

It's indisputable that the lives of people across the world have changed (for better or for worse is an entirely different discussion) with the introduction of the personal computing experience. Take a full week and start a running tally of how many hours you spend using a computer, listening to music on a digital device, operating a smartphone. Directly or indirectly, Steve Jobs pushed the world forcefully in the direction he wanted it to go. He may not have been the inventor of any of the devices or programs that have come to be synonymously associated with Steve Jobs. But his genius was in understanding and anticipating what people wanted before they knew it even existed (there are more than a few quotes in this collection relaying that exact sentiment).

Henry David Thoreau said that he wanted to "live deep and suck out all the marrow of life . . . to put to rout all that was not life . . . and not, when [he] came to die, discover [he] had not lived." Clearly, when Steve Jobs finally succumbed to pancreatic cancer at the age of 56, no one could question whether he had sucked the marrow out of life. He continued to lead Apple and mankind into the future almost until the day he died. He was as unique as he was private, both as an individual and as the public face of Apple Inc. You may not be surprised to find that the number of interviews he granted since 1976 is limited. But what touched me, and will hopefully leave its mark on you, is how much he was able to convey in such a short time span. His 2005 commencement address at Stanford University could serve as a standalone piece of literature.

As many have pointed out, it's rare that one man represents the public face of a company to the extent that Steve Jobs did for Apple. Maybe that's why so many took it so personally upon hearing the news of his passing. It wasn't because he was a particularly kind or generous man (as you'll see hints of throughout this book). It wasn't because Apple's products were perfect (they weren't, and you'll see some of that here too). Maybe, just maybe, it was because for the past ten years we've all relied on Steve to show us what's next, to let us know where we're heading and what we're going to need to get us there. It could be that we're all subconsciously fanboys, whether we want to admit it or not.

Stock in Apple took a temporary dip immediately following his death and I'd like to think, romantically, that for the first time in a decade there was a brief but unified moment as the world, suddenly unsure of the future, faltered as it took its first steps without him.

—A.K.T., 2011

On Beginnings

"We started off with a very idealistic perspective—that doing something with the highest quality, doing it right the first time, would really be cheaper than having to go back and do it again."

—*Newsweek*, 1984

"Silicon Valley for the most part at that time was still orchards—apricot orchards and prune orchards—and it was really paradise. I remember the air being crystal clear, where you could see from one end of the valley to the other."

—On growing up in Silicon Valley in the early 1960s,

Smithsonian Institution, 1995

"Things became much more clear that they were the results of human creation, not these magical things that just appeared in one's environment that one had no knowledge of their interiors. It gave a tremendous level of self-confidence, that through exploration and learning one could understand seemingly very complex things in one's environment. My childhood was very fortunate in that way."

—Smithsonian Institution, 1995

"When we finally presented [the Macintosh desktop computer] at the shareholders' meeting, everyone in the auditorium gave it a five-minute ovation. What was incredible to me was that I could see the Mac team in the first few rows. It was as though none of us could believe we'd actually finished it. Everyone started crying."

—*Playboy*, 1985

"Usually it takes ten years and a 100 million dollars to associate a symbol with the name of the company. Our challenge was how could we have a little jewel that we could use without a name to put on the product?"

—1993 interview about the famous Apple logo

"'I was in the parking lot, with the key in the car, and I thought to myself, If this is my last night on earth, would I rather spend it at a business meeting or with this woman? I ran across the parking lot, asked her if she'd have dinner with me. She said yes, we walked into town and we've been together ever since."

—On meeting his wife, Laurene, *The New York Times*, 1997

"The people who built Silicon Valley were engineers. They learned business, they learned a lot of different things, but they had a real belief that humans, if they worked hard with other creative, smart people, could solve most of humankind's problems. I believe that very much."

—*Wired*, 1996

"One of the things I did when I got back to Apple 10 years ago was I gave the museum to Stanford and all the papers and all the old machines and kind of cleared out the cobwebs and said, let's stop looking backwards here. It's all about what happens tomorrow."

—All Things Digital D5 conference, 2007

"From almost the beginning at Apple we were, for some incredibly lucky reason, fortunate enough to be at the right place at the right time."

"I had dinner in Seattle at Bill Gates' house a couple of weeks ago. We were both remarking how at one time we were the youngest guys in this business, and now we're the graybeards."

"So we went to Atari and said, 'Hey, we've got this amazing thing, even built with some of your parts, and what do you think about funding us? Or we'll give it to you. We just want to do it. Pay our salary, we'll come work for you.' And they said, 'No.' So then we went to Hewlett-Packard, and they said, 'Hey, we don't need you. You haven't got through college yet.'"

"I think this is the start of something really big. Sometimes that first step is the hardest one, and we've just taken it."

"I was lucky—I found what I love to do early in life."

"[Apple co-founder Steve Wozniak] and I very much like Bob Dylan's poetry, and we spent a lot of time thinking about a lot of that stuff. This was California. You could get LSD fresh made from Stanford. You could sleep on the beach at night with your girlfriend. California has a sense of experimentation and a sense of openness—openness to new possibilities."

—*Playboy*, 1985

"You saw the 1984 commercial. Macintosh was basically this relatively small company in Cupertino, California, taking on the goliath, IBM, and saying, 'Wait a minute, your way is wrong. This is not the way we want computers to go. This is not the legacy we want to leave. This is not what we want our kids to be learning. This is wrong and we are going to show you the right way to do it and here it is. It's called Macintosh and it is so much better. It's going to beat you and you're going to do it.'"

—Smithsonian Institution, 1995

On Business

"You can't just ask customers what they want and then try to give that to them. By the time you get it built, they'll want something new."

—*Inc.,* 1989

"Quality is more important than quantity. One home run is much better than two doubles."

—*BusinessWeek,* 2006

"Apple has some tremendous assets, but I believe without some attention, the company could, could, could—I'm searching for the right word—could, could die."

—*Time*, 1997, on his return to Apple as CEO

"The cure for Apple is not cost-cutting. The cure for Apple is to innovate its way out of its current predicament."

—*Apple Confidential 2.0: The Definitive History of the World's Most Colorful Company* (2004)

by Owen W. Linzmayer

"That's been one of my mantras—focus and simplicity. Simple can be harder than complex: You have to work hard to get your thinking clean to make it simple. But it's worth it in the end because once you get there, you can move mountains."

—*BusinessWeek*, 1998

"You know, we don't have a belief that the Mac is going to take over 80 percent of the PC market."

"You can't really predict exactly what will happen, but you can feel the direction that we're going. And that's about as close as you can get. Then you just stand back and get out of the way, and these things take on a life of their own."

—*Rolling Stone*, 1994

"We're gambling on our vision, and we would rather do that than make 'me too' products. Let some other companies do that. For us, it's always the next dream."

—Interview for the release of the Macintosh, 1984

"Be a yardstick of quality. Some people aren't used to an environment where excellence is expected."

"If copyright dies, if patents die, if the protection of intellectual property is eroded, then people will stop investing. That hurts everyone."

—*Rolling Stone*, 2003

"We're not just building a computer, we're building a company."

—*Esquire*, 1986

"Apple is a company that doesn't have the most resources of everybody in the world. The way we've succeeded is by choosing what horses to ride really carefully . . . we're organized like a startup. We're the biggest startup on the planet."

—All Things Digital D8 conference, 2010

"If Mercedes made a bicycle or a hamburger or a computer, I don't think there'd be much advantage in having its logo on it. I don't think Apple would get much equity putting its name on an automobile, either. And just because the whole world is going digital—TV, audio, and all that—doesn't mean there's anything wrong with just being in the computer business. The computer business is huge."

—*Fortune*, 1998

"You need a very product-oriented culture, even in a technology company. Lots of companies have tons of great engineers and smart people. But ultimately, there needs to be some gravitational force that pulls it all together. Otherwise, you can get great pieces of technology all floating around the universe."

—*Newsweek*, 2004

"I think the way out is not to slash and burn, it's to innovate. That's how Apple got to its glory, and that's how Apple could return to it."

—*Wall $treet Week*, 1996

"You can't look back and say, well, gosh, you know, I wish I hadn't have gotten fired, I wish I was there, I wish this, I wish that. It doesn't matter. And so let's go invent tomorrow rather than worrying about what happened yesterday."

—All Things Digital D5 conference, 2007

"The system is that there is no system. That doesn't mean we don't have process. Apple is a very disciplined company, and we have great processes. But that's not what it's about. Process makes you more efficient."

—*Newsweek*, 2004

"There were 15 product lines when I got here. It was incredible. You couldn't figure out what to buy. I started asking around, and nobody could explain it to me."

—On returning to Apple

"The subscription model of buying music is bankrupt. I think you could make available the Second Coming in a subscription model and it might not be successful."

—*Rolling Stone*, 2003

"I've always wanted to own and control the primary technology in everything we do."

—*BusinessWeek*, 2004

"There were some very hard decisions to make. Like the decision to end the clone business. In hindsight that looks smart, but have you ever gotten death threats? That was scary."

—On making hard changes to Apple when he returned as CEO

"I think if you do something and it turns out pretty good, then you should go do something else wonderful, not dwell on it for too long. Just figure out what's next."

—MSNBC, 2006

"Just avoid holding it in that way."

—Personal e-mail to a customer with concerns over an antenna reception issue with the newly released iPhone 4, where calls were dropped when the user grasped the product's steel-banded sides, 2010

"I think building a company's really hard, and it requires your greatest persuasive abilities to hire the best people you can and keep them at your company and keep them working, doing the best work of their lives, hopefully."

—All Things Digital D5 conference, 2007

"I used to be the youngest guy in every meeting I was in, and now I'm usually the oldest. And the older I get, the more I'm convinced that motives make so much difference."

—*BusinessWeek*, 2004

"I think it's really hard for one company to do everything. Life's complex."

—All Things Digital D5 conference, 2007

"There are sneakers that cost more than an iPod."
—On the iPod's $300 price tag, *Newsweek*, 2003

"Well, you know us. We never talk about future products. There used to be a saying at Apple: Isn't it funny? A ship that leaks from the top. So—I don't wanna perpetuate that. So I really can't say."
—On any information regarding upcoming iPod releases, *ABC News*, 2005

"I don't think in terms of market shares, I think in terms of us making the best personal computers in the world, and if we can do that, I think our market share will go up."

—CNA, 1999

"To me, the company is one of humanity's most amazing inventions."

—*Fortune*, 1998

"A lot of companies have chosen to downsize, and maybe that was the right thing for them. We chose a different path. Our belief was that if we kept putting great products in front of customers, they would continue to open their wallets."

"It wasn't that Microsoft was so brilliant or clever in copying the Mac, it's that the Mac was a sitting duck for 10 years. That's Apple's problem: Their differentiation evaporated."

"If I were running Apple, I would milk the Macintosh for all it's worth—and get busy on the next great thing. The PC wars are over. Done. Microsoft won a long time ago."

—*Fortune*, 1996

"To turn really interesting ideas and fledgling technologies into a company that can continue to innovate for years, it requires a lot of disciplines."

"So how do you communicate to people that they are in an environment where excellence is expected? You don't say it. You don't put it in an employee handbook. That stuff is meaningless. All that counts is the product that results from the work of the group. That will say more than anything coming out of your mouth or your pen."

"I've also found that the best companies pay attention
to aesthetics. They take the extra time to lay out grids
and proportion things appropriately, and it seems to pay
off for them. I mean, beyond the functional benefits, the
aesthetic communicates something about how they think of
themselves, their sense of discipline in engineering, how they
run their company, stuff like that."

—*Inc.*, 1989

"Customers think the price is really good where it is. We're trying to compete with piracy—we're trying to pull people away from piracy and say, 'You can buy these songs legally for a fair price.' But if the price goes up a lot, they'll go back to piracy. Then, everybody loses."

"The HD revolution is over, it happened. HD won. Everybody wants HD."

—Apple Special Event keynote, 2010

"A lot of people can't get past the fact that we're not going after the enterprise market. But that's like saying, 'How can the Gap be successful not making suits?' Well, we don't make wingtips here either."

—*Fortune,* 2000

"In business, if I knew earlier what I know now, I'd have probably done some things a lot better than I did, but I also would've probably done some other things a lot worse. But so what? It's more important to be engaged in the present."

—*Fortune,* 1998

"If I give you 20 bricks, you could lay them all on the ground and you'd have 20 bricks on the ground. Or you can lay them on top of each other and start building a wall."

"We hire people who want to make the best things in the world."

"Technology is nothing. What's important is that you have a faith in people, that they're basically good and smart, and if you give them tools, they'll do wonderful things with them."

—*Rolling Stone*, 1994

"And boy, have we patented it!"

—Introducing the iPhone, *Macworld*, 2007

"Do your best at every job. Don't sleep! Success generates more success so be hungry for it. Hire good people with a passion for excellence."

"You make some of the best products in the world—but you also make a lot of crap. Get rid of the crappy stuff."

—As said to Nike

"There were too many people at Apple and in the Apple ecosystem playing the game of, for Apple to win, Microsoft has to lose. And it was clear that you didn't have to play that game because Apple wasn't going to beat Microsoft. Apple didn't have to beat Microsoft. Apple had to remember who Apple was because they'd forgotten who Apple was."

—All Things Digital D5 conference, 2007

On Leadership

"My job is to not be easy on people. My job is to make them better."

"When I hire somebody really senior, competence is the ante. They have to be really smart. But the real issue for me is, Are they going to fall in love with Apple? Because if they fall in love with Apple, everything else will take care of itself."

—*Fortune*, 2008

"This is not a one-man show."

—BusinessWeek, 1998

"My number one job here at Apple is to make sure that the top 100 people are A+ players. And everything else will take care of itself."

—Time, 1999

"I'm a very big believer in equal opportunity as opposed to equal outcome. I don't believe in equal outcome because unfortunately life's not like that. It would be a pretty boring place if it was."

—*Computerworld* Smithsonian Awards, 1995

"We all tend to reduce reality to symbols, but Superman went out a long time ago. The way you accomplish anything significant is with a team."

—*Inc.*, 1989

"My model for business is the Beatles. They were four guys who kept each other's kind of negative tendencies in check. They balanced each other and the total was greater than the sum of the parts. That's how I see business: great things in business are never done by one person, they're done by a team of people."

—*60 Minutes*, 2003

"I know people like symbols, but it's always unsettling when people write stories about me, because they tend to overlook a lot of other people."

—*Time*, 1999

"Some people say, 'Oh, God, if Jobs got run over by a bus, Apple would be in trouble.' And, you know, I think it wouldn't be a party, but there are really capable people at Apple. And the board would have some good choices about who to pick as CEO."

—*Fortune*, 2008

"The people who are doing the work are the moving force behind the Macintosh. My job is to create a space for them, to clear out the rest of the organization and keep it at bay."

"The things that I have done in my life, I think the things we do now at Pixar, these are team sports. They are not something one person does."

—*Charlie Rose*, 1996

On Innovation

"Innovation distinguishes between a leader and a follower."

"Every once in a while a revolutionary product comes along that changes everything. It's very fortunate if you can work on just one of these in your career. . . . Apple's been very fortunate in that it's introduced a few of these."
—Apple press release for the release of the iPhone, 2007

"Everyone wants a MacBook Pro because they are so bitchin."

—Apple shareholder meeting, 2006

"We believe it's the biggest advance in animation since Walt Disney started it all with the release of Snow White 50 years ago."

—*Fortune*, 1995, on *Toy Story*

"Apple's the only PC company left that makes the whole widget—hardware and software. That means Apple can really decide that it will make a system dramatically easier to use, which is a great asset when you're going after consumers."

"iMac is next year's computer for $1,299, not last year's computer for $999."

—Introducing the first iMac computer, 1998

"It's not about pop culture, and it's not about fooling people, and it's not about convincing people that they want something they don't. We figure out what we want."

—*Fortune*, 2008

"It's really hard to design products by focus groups. A lot of times, people don't know what they want until you show it to them."

—*BusinessWeek*, 1998

"A creative period like this lasts only maybe a decade, but it can be a golden decade if we manage it properly."

—Following the release of the iMac, *Fortune*, 2000

"What we want to do is make a leapfrog product that is way smarter than any mobile device has ever been, and super-easy to use. This is what iPhone is. OK? So, we're going to reinvent the phone."

"Innovation has nothing to do with how many R&D dollars you have. When Apple came up with the Mac, IBM was spending at least 100 times more on R&D. It's not about money. It's about the people you have, how you're led, and how much you get it."

—*Fortune*, 1998

"It was a great challenge. Let's make a great phone that we fall in love with."

"The broader one's understanding of the human experience, the better design we will have."

"Creativity is just connecting things. When you ask creative people how they did something, they feel a little guilty because they didn't really do it, they just saw something. It seemed obvious to them after a while. That's because they were able to connect experiences they've had and synthesize new things."

"And [innovation] comes from saying no to 1,000 things to make sure we don't get on the wrong track or try to do too much. We're always thinking about new markets we could enter, but it's only by saying no that you can concentrate on the things that are really important."

—*BusinessWeek*, 2004

"Take desktop video editing. I never got one request from someone who wanted to edit movies on his computer. Yet now that people see it, they say, 'Oh my God, that's great!'"

—*Fortune*, 2000

"It's rare that you see an artist in his 30s or 40s able to really contribute something amazing."

—*Playboy*, 1985

"People think it's this veneer—that the designers are handed this box and told, 'Make it look good!' That's not what we think design is. It's not just what it looks like and feels like. Design is how it works."

—*The New York Times*, 2003

"The products suck! There's no sex in them anymore!"

—On the state of Apple just before his return,

BusinessWeek, 1997

"You know, you keep on innovating, you keep on making better stuff. And if you always want the latest and greatest, then you have to buy a new iPod at least once a year."

—MSNBC, 2006

"We're trying to make great products for people, and we at least have the courage of our convictions to say 'We don't think this is part of what makes a great product, we're going to leave it out.' That's what a lot of customers pay us to do."

—All Things Digital D5 conference, 2010

"When you're a carpenter making a beautiful chest of drawers, you're not going to use a piece of plywood on the back, even though it faces the wall and nobody will ever see it. You'll know it's there, so you're going to use a beautiful piece of wood on the back. For you to sleep well at night, the aesthetic, the quality, has to be carried all the way through."

"Innovation comes from people meeting up in the hallways or calling each other at 10:30 at night with a new idea, or because they realized something that shoots holes in how we've been thinking about a problem."

—*Businessweek*, 2004

"Don't take it all too seriously. If you want to live your life in a creative way, as an artist, you have to not look back too much. You have to be willing to take whatever you've done and whoever you were and throw them away."

—*Playboy*, 1985

"We cook up new products. You never really know If people will love them as much as you do. The most exciting thing is you have butterflies in your stomach in the days leading up to these events."

—CNBC, 2007

"Sometimes when you innovate, you make mistakes. It is best to admit them quickly, and get on with improving your other innovations."

"Take the iPhone. We had a different enclosure design for this iPhone until way too close to the introduction to ever change it. And I came in one Monday morning, I said, 'I just don't love this. I can't convince myself to fall in love with this. And this is the most important product we've ever done.' And we pushed the reset button."

—*Fortune*, 2008

"The design of the Mac wasn't what it looked like, although that was part of it. Primarily, it was how it worked. To design something really well, you have to get it."

"The reason we wouldn't make a seven-inch tablet isn't because we don't want to hit a price point, it's because we don't think you can make a great tablet with a seven-inch screen."

"There's no other company that could make a MacBook Air and the reason is that not only do we control the hardware, but we control the operating system. And it is the intimate interaction between the operating system and the hardware that allows us to do that. There is no intimate interaction between Windows and a Dell notebook."

"You've got to start with the customer experience and work back toward the technology—not the other way around."
—Apple Worldwide Developers Conference, 1997

"The desktop computer industry is dead. Innovation has virtually ceased. Microsoft dominates with very little innovation. That's over. Apple lost. The desktop market has entered the dark ages, and it's going to be in the dark ages for the next 10 years, or certainly for the rest of this decade."

—*Wired*, 1996

"There's an old Wayne Gretzky quote that I love. 'I skate to where the puck is going to be, not where it has been.' And we've always tried to do that at Apple. Since the very very beginning. And we always will."

"You know, I've got a plan that could rescue Apple. I can't say any more than that it's the perfect product and the perfect strategy for Apple. But nobody there will listen to me . . ."

—*Fortune*, 1995

"They really thought the process through. They did such a great job designing these washers and dryers. I got more thrill out of them than I have out of any piece of high tech in years."

—On Miele, a Germany-based manufacturer of high-end domestic appliances, *Wired*, 1996

"Who wants a stylus? You have to get 'em and put 'em away and you lose 'em. Yuck. Nobody wants a stylus."

"We have some pretty cool stuff coming, but we don't talk about it."

—*BusinessWeek*, 1998

On Everyone Else

"The only problem with Microsoft is they just have no taste, they have absolutely no taste. . . . I guess I am saddened, not by Microsoft's success—I have no problem with their success, they've earned their success for the most part. I have a problem with the fact that they just make really third-rate products."

—PBS documentary *Triumph of the Nerds*, 1996

"I told him I believed every word of what I'd said but that I never should have said it in public."

—On apologizing to Bill Gates for disparaging Microsoft in a documentary, *The New York Times*, 1997

"Nobody has tried to swallow us since I've been here. I think they are afraid how we would taste."

—*BusinessWeek*, 1998

"With our technology, with objects, literally three people in a garage can blow away what 200 people at Microsoft can do."

"Bill Gates'd be a broader guy if he had dropped acid once or gone off to an ashram when he was younger."

—*The New York Times*, 1997

"Unfortunately, people are not rebelling against Microsoft. They don't know any better."

—*Rolling Stone*, 1994

"We've also both been incredibly lucky to have had great partners that we started the companies with and we've attracted great people. I mean, so everything that's been done at Microsoft and at Apple has been done by just remarkable people, none of which are sitting up here today."

—On Microsoft, All Things Digital D5 conference, 2007

"I've seen the demonstrations on the Internet about how you can find another person using a Zune and give them a song they can play three times. It takes forever. By the time you've gone through all that, the girl's got up and left! You're much better off to take one of your ear buds out and put it in her ear. Then you're connected with about two feet of headphone cable."

—On competition between the iPod and Microsoft's Zune,

Newsweek, 2006

"The problem with the Internet startup craze isn't that too many people are starting companies; it's that too many people aren't sticking with it. That's somewhat understandable, because there are many moments that are filled with despair and agony, when you have to fire people and cancel things and deal with very difficult situations. That's when you find out who you are and what your values are."

—*Fortune*, 2000

"It's like giving a glass of ice water to somebody in hell!"

—On iTunes being one of the largest software developers for Windows OS, All Things Digital D5 conference, 2007

"They are shamelessly copying us."

—On the development of Microsoft's Vista operating system, *CNET News*, 2005

"They're all putting their dumb controls in the shape of a circle, to fool the consumer into thinking it's a wheel like ours. We've sort of set the vernacular. They're trying to copy the vernacular without understanding it."

—On companies making iPod lookalikes,

The New York Times, 2003

"When the Internet came along and Napster came along, people in the music business didn't know what to make of the changes. A lot of these folks didn't use computers, weren't on e-mail—didn't really know what Napster was for a few years. They were pretty doggone slow to react. Matter of fact, they still haven't really reacted."

—*Rolling Stone*, 2003

"The engineering is long gone in most PC companies. In the consumer electronics companies, they don't understand the software parts of it. And so you really can't make the products that you can make at Apple anywhere else right now. Apple's the only company that has everything under one roof."

—*Fortune*, 2008

"The relationship between the Mac development team at Microsoft and Apple is a great relationship. It's one of our best developer relationships."

"So when these people sell out, even though they get fabulously rich, they're gypping themselves out of one of the potentially most rewarding experiences of their unfolding lives. Without it, they may never know their values or how to keep their newfound wealth in perspective."

"Pretty much, Apple and Dell are the only ones in this industry making money. They make it by being Wal-Mart. We make it by innovation."

"This is a story that's amazing. It's got theft, it's got buying stolen property, it's got extortion. I'm sure it's got sex in there somewhere. Somebody should make a movie out of this!"

—On the circumstances surrounding an iPhone prototype that was discovered in a bar and published in an online technology blog, Gizmodo, All Things Digital D8 Conference 2010

"Our friends up north spend over five billion dollars on research and development and all they seem to do is copy Google and Apple."

—On Microsoft, Apple Worldwide Developer's Conference, 2006

"Japan's very interesting. Some people think it copies things. I don't think that anymore. I think what they do is reinvent things. They will get something that's already been invented and study it until they thoroughly understand it. In some cases, they understand it better than the original inventor."

"Microsoft has had two goals in the last 10 years. One was to copy the Mac, and the other was to copy Lotus' success in the spreadsheet—basically, the applications business. And over the course of the last 10 years, Microsoft accomplished both of those goals. And now they are completely lost."

"Bill built the first software company in the industry and I think he built the first software company before anybody really in our industry knew what a software company was, except for these guys. And that was huge. That was really huge."

—On Bill Gates, All Things Digital D5 conference, 2007

"You think I'm an arrogant [expletive] who thinks he's above the law, and I think you're a slime bucket who gets most of his facts wrong."

—To a *New York Times* reporter who asked about Jobs' health, 2008

"It's like when IBM drove a lot of innovation out of the computer industry before the microprocessor came along. Eventually, Microsoft will crumble because of complacency, and maybe some new things will grow. But until that happens, until there's some fundamental technology shift, it's just over."

—*Wired*, 1996

On Technology

"The Web is not going to change the world, certainly not in the next 10 years. It's going to augment the world."

—*Wired*, 1996

"For me, the most exciting thing in the software area is the Internet, and part of the reason for that is no one owns it. It's a free for all, it's much like the early days of the personal computer."

—*Wall $treet Week*, 1995

"It'll make your jaw drop."

—On the first NeXT computer, *The New York Times*, 1989

"Computers are the first thing to come along since books that will sit there and interact with you endlessly, without judgment."

—*Playboy*, 1985

"Customers can't anticipate what the technology can do."

—*Inc.*, 1989

"I love things that level hierarchy, that bring the individual up to the same level as an organization, or a small group up to the same level as a large group with much greater resources. And the Web and the Internet do that. It's a very profound thing."

—*Wired*, 1996

"A computer is the most incredible tool we've ever seen. It can be a writing tool, a communications center, a supercalculator, a planner, a filer and an artistic instrument all in one, just by being given new instructions, or software, to work from. There are no other tools that have the power and versatility of a computer."

—*Playboy*, 1985

"Older people sit down and ask, 'What is it?' but the boy asks, 'What can I do with it?'"

"I think humans are basically tool builders, and the computer is the most remarkable tool we've ever built. The big insight a lot of us had in the 1970s had to do with the importance of putting that tool in the hands of individuals."

—*Inc.*, 1989

"We're getting to the point where everything's a computer in a different form factor. So what, right? So what if it's built with a computer inside it? It doesn't matter. It's, what is it? How do you use it? You know, how does the consumer approach it? And so who cares what's inside it anymore?"

—All Things Digital D5 conference, 2007

"People are inherently creative. They will use tools in ways the toolmakers never thought possible."

—*Inc.*, 1989

"I think it's brought the world a lot closer together, and will continue to do that. There are downsides to everything; there are unintended consequences to everything. The most corrosive piece of technology that I've ever seen is called television—but then, again, television, at its best, is magnificent."

—*Rolling Stone*, 2003

"The most exciting things happening today are objects and the Web. The Web is exciting for two reasons. One, it's ubiquitous. There will be Web dial tone everywhere. And anything that's ubiquitous gets interesting. Two, I don't think Microsoft will figure out a way to own it. There's going to be a lot more innovation, and that will create a place where there isn't this dark cloud of dominance."

—*Wired*, 1996

"A lot of people are starting to feel that having a personal computer, especially one that is able to deliver as robust an Internet experience as the iMac can in the home, is an essential utility."

—*BusinessWeek*, 1998

"If you look at things I've done in my life, they have an element of democratizing. The Web is an incredible democratizer. A small company can look as large as a big company and be as accessible as a big company on the Web. Big companies spend hundreds of millions of dollars building their distribution channels. And the Web is going to completely neutralize that advantage."

—*Wired*, 1996

"The Apple II peeled off the hardware layer. You didn't need to know about the hardware to use a computer. The next step was the transition from the Apple II to the Macintosh, which peeled off the computer-literacy layer, if you will. In other words, you didn't have to be a hacker or a computer scientist to use one of these."

—*Inc.*, 1989

"We think basically you watch television to turn your brain off, and you work on your computer when you want to turn your brain on."

—*Macworld*, 2004

"What we can put in a computer for $1,000 is just mind-blowing."

"Computers themselves, and software yet to be developed, will revolutionize the way we learn."

"It takes these very simple-minded instructions—'Go fetch a number, add it to this number, put the result there, perceive if it's greater than this other number'—but executes them at a rate of, let's say, 1,000,000 per second. At 1,000,000 per second, the results appear to be magic."

—Explaining the first computers

"What a computer is to me is the most remarkable tool that we have ever come up with. It's the equivalent of a bicycle for our minds."

—*Memory and Imagination: New Pathways to the Library of Congress* (1991)

"You'll see more and more perfection of that—computer as servant. But the next thing is going to be computer as a guide or agent."

"The most compelling reason for most people to buy a computer for the home will be to link it into a nationwide communications network. We're just in the beginning stages of what will be a truly remarkable breakthrough for most people—as remarkable as the telephone."

"These technologies can make life easier, can let us touch people we might not otherwise. You may have a child with a birth defect and be able to get in touch with other parents and support groups, get medical information, the latest experimental drugs. These things can profoundly influence life. I'm not downplaying that."

On Drive

"I think I have five more great products in me."

—*Esquire*, 1986

"Because I'm the CEO, and I think it can be done."

—On why he chose to override engineers who
thought the iMac wasn't feasible, *Time*, 2005

"Whenever you do any one thing intensely over a period of time, you have to give up other lives you could be living. You have to have a real single-minded kind of tunnel vision if you want to get anything significant accomplished. Especially if the desire is not to be a businessman, but to be a creative person."

—*Esquire*, 1986

"We're the last guys left in this industry who can do it, and that's what we're about."

"Our goal is to make the best devices in the world, not to be the biggest."

—Conference call with analysts, 2010

"Our DNA is as a consumer company—for that individual customer who's voting thumbs up or thumbs down. That's who we think about. And we think that our job is to take responsibility for the complete user experience. And if it's not up to par, it's our fault, plain and simply."

"We believe that customers are smart, and want objects which are well thought through."

"Remembering that you are going to die is the best way I know to avoid the trap of thinking you have something to lose. You are already naked. There is no reason not to follow your heart."

"You just make the best product you can, and you don't put it out until you feel it's right. But no matter what you think intellectually, your heart is beating pretty fast right before people see what you've produced."

"If they keep on risking failure, they're still artists. Dylan and Picasso were always risking failure."

"Leonardo da Vinci was a great artist and a great scientist. Michelangelo knew a tremendous amount about how to cut stone at the quarry. The finest dozen computer scientists I know are all musicians."

"I have a great respect for incremental improvement, and I've done that sort of thing in my life, but I've always been attracted to the more revolutionary changes. I don't know why. Because they're harder. They're much more stressful emotionally. And you usually go through a period where everybody tells you that you've completely failed."

"We don't get a chance to do that many things, and every one should be really excellent. Because this is our life. Life is brief, and then you die . . . And we've all chosen to do this with our lives. So it better be damn good. It better be worth it."

—*Fortune*

"We want to stand at the intersection of computers and humanism."

"Why music? Well, we love music and it's always good to do something you love."

—Introducing the first iPod, 2001

"We think the Mac will sell zillions, but we didn't build the Mac for anybody else. We built it for ourselves."

"We're still heavily into the box. We love the box. […] I still spend a lot of my time working on new computers, and it will always be a primal thing for Apple. But the user experience is what we care about most, and we're expanding that experience beyond the box by making better use of the Internet."

—*Fortune*, 2000

"The worst thing that could possibly happen as we get big and we get a little bit more influence in the world is if we change our core values and start letting it slide. I can't do that. I'd rather quit. We have the same values now as we had then."

—On whether the company should have gone after Gizmodo,

All Things Digital D8 conference, 2010

"There's a very strong DNA within Apple, and that's about taking state-of-the-art technology and making it easy for people."

—*Guardian*, 2005

"My position coming back to Apple was that our industry was in a coma. It reminded me of Detroit in the 70s, when American cars were boats on wheels."

"Everyone here has the sense that right now is one of those moments when we are influencing the future."

"People say you have to have a lot of passion for what you're doing and it's totally true. And the reason is because it's so hard that if you don't, any rational person would give up."
—All Things Digital D5 conference, 2007

"I'm convinced that about half of what separates the successful entrepreneurs from the non-successful ones is pure perseverance. It is so hard. You put so much of your life into this thing."

—*Computerworld* Smithsonian Awards, 1995

"You've got to be careful choosing what you're going to do. Once you pick something you really care about, and it's a worthwhile thing to do, then you can kind of forget about it and just work at it. The dedication comes naturally."

—*Fortune,* 1998

"I've worked my tail off here. I don't think I could work any harder."

—*BusinessWeek*, 1998

"We're just enthusiastic about what we do."

"It's hard to tell with these Internet startups if they're really interested in building companies or if they're just interested in the money. I can tell you, though: If they don't really want to build a company, they won't luck into it. That's because it's so hard that if you don't have a passion, you'll give up."

—*Fortune*, 2000

On Legacy

"It will go down in history as a turning point for the music industry. This is landmark stuff. I can't overestimate it!"

—On the iPod and the iTunes music store, *Fortune*, 2003

"Pixar is making art for the ages. Kids will be watching *Toy Story* in the future. And Apple is much more of a constant race to continually improve things and stay ahead of the competition."

—*Time*, 1999

"Being the richest man in the cemetery doesn't matter to me . . . Going to bed at night saying we've done something wonderful . . . that's what matters to me."

—*Wall Street Journal*, 1993

"Each year has been so robust with problems and successes and learning experiences and human experiences that a year is a lifetime at Apple."

"Pixar is the most technically advanced creative company; Apple is the most creatively advanced technical company."

—*Fortune*, 2005

"That's why I love what we do—we make these tools and they're constantly surprising us."

—All Things Digital D5 conference, 2007

"We used to dream about this stuff. Now we get to build it. It's pretty great."

—Keynote address, Apple Worldwide Development
Conference, 2004

"Things don't have to change the world to be important."

—*Wired*, 2006

"And no, we don't know where it will lead. We just know there's something much bigger than any of us here."

"Apple really beats to a different drummer. I used to say that Apple should be the Sony of this business, but in reality, I think Apple should be the Apple of this business."

—*BusinessWeek*, 1998

"We are guilty as charged of making mistakes, because nobody's ever done this before."

—On Apple's App Store's policy for rejection,
All Things Digital D8 conference, 2010

"Apple is a $30 billion company, yet we've got less than 30 major products. I don't know if that's ever been done before."

"If you go out and ask people what's wrong with computers today, they'll tell you they're really complicated, they have a zillion cables coming out of the back, they're really big and noisy, they're really ugly, and they take forever to get on the Internet. And so we tried to set out to fix those problems with products like the iMac."

—CNA, 1999

"The buying experience and ownership experience of owning a Mac is maybe the best of any product I know."

—CNBC, 2006

"It took us three years to build the NeXT computer. If we'd given customers what they said they wanted, we'd have built a computer they'd have been happy with a year after we spoke to them—not something they'd want now."

"That same innovation, that same engineering, that same talent applied where we don't run up against the fact that Microsoft got this monopoly, and boom! We have 75 percent market share."

—On the iPod's success

"I don't think that people have special responsibilities just because they've done something that other people like or don't like. I think the work speaks for itself."

—Smithsonian Institution, 1995

"Apple's market share is bigger than BMW's or Mercedes's or Porsche's in the automotive market. What's wrong with being BMW or Mercedes?"

"I get asked a lot why Apple's customers are so loyal. It's not because they belong to the Church of Mac! That's ridiculous."

"I'm as proud of what we don't do as I am of what we do."

—*BusinessWeek*

"Most people have no concept of how an automatic transmission works, yet they know how to drive a car. You don't have to study physics to understand the laws of motion to drive a car. You don't have to understand any of this stuff to use Macintosh."

"Now, we are selling over 5 million songs a day now. Isn't that unbelievable? That's 58 songs every second of every minute of every hour of every day."

"So let's not use a stylus. We're going to use the best pointing device in the world. We're going to use a pointing device that we're all born with—born with ten of them. We're going to use our fingers. We're going to touch this with our fingers. And we have invented a new technology called multi-touch, which is phenomenal. It works like magic."

"Picasso had a saying: 'Good artists copy, great artists steal.'
We have always been shameless about stealing great ideas . . .
I think part of what made the Macintosh great was that the
people working on it were musicians, poets, artists, zoologists,
and historians who also happened to be the best computer
scientists in the world."

—Interview, 1994

"There's nothing that makes my day more than getting an
e-mail from some random person in the universe who just
bought an iPad over in the UK and tells me the story about
how it's the coolest product they've ever brought home in
their lives. That's what keeps me going."

"Apple turns out many products—a dozen a year; if you count all the minor ones, probably a hundred. Pixar is striving to turn out one a year. But the converse of that is that Pixar's products will still be used fifty years from now, whereas I don't think you'll be using any product Apple brings to market this year fifty years from now."

—*Time*, 1999

"John Sculley ruined Apple and he ruined it by bringing a set of values to the top of Apple which were corrupt and corrupted some of the top people who were there, drove out some of the ones who were not corruptible, and brought in more corrupt ones and paid themselves collectively tens of millions of dollars and cared more about their own glory and wealth than they did about what built Apple in the first place—which was making great computers for people to use."

—*Computerworld* Smithsonian Awards Program, 1995

"We've gone through the operating system and looked at everything and asked how can we simplify this and make it more powerful at the same time."

"We made the buttons on the screen look so good you'll want to lick them."

—*Fortune*, 2000

"Click. Boom. Amazing!"

—Macworld keynote address, 2006

"I've had lots of girlfriends. But the greatest high in my life was the day we introduced the Macintosh."

—*Esquire*, 1986

On Life

"I would trade all of my technology for an afternoon with Socrates."
—*Newsweek*, 2001

"Your time is limited, so don't waste it living someone else's life . . . Don't let the noise of other's opinions drown out your own inner voice. And most important, have the courage to follow your heart and intuition. They somehow already know what you truly want to become."
—Stanford University commencement address, 2005

"It's more fun to be a pirate than to join the navy."

—*Odyssey: Pepsi to Apple*, 1982

"You can tell a lot about a person by who his or her heroes are."

—*BusinessWeek*, 2004

"The ones who are crazy enough to think that they can change the world, are the ones who do."

—"Think Different" promotional video by Apple, 1997

"I'm the only person I know that's lost a quarter of a billion dollars in one year. . . . It's very character-building."

—*Apple Confidential 2.0: The Definitive History of the World's Most Colorful Company* (2004) by Owen W. Linzmayer

"Sometimes life hits you in the head with a brick. Don't lose faith."

"Just to try to be as good a father to them as my father was to me. I think about that every day of my life."

—On raising his children, *The New York Times*, 1997

"I make fifty cents for showing up . . . and the other fifty cents is based on my performance."

—Apple shareholder meeting, 2007, on his annual salary of $1

"You have no reason not to follow your heart."

"I was worth about over a million dollars when I was twenty-three and over ten million dollars when I was twenty-four, and over a hundred million dollars when I was twenty-five and it wasn't that important because I never did it for the money."

—*Triumph of the Nerds*, 1996

"The only way to do great work is to love what you do. If you haven't found it yet, keep looking. Don't settle. As with all matters of the heart, you'll know when you find it."

—Stanford University commencement address, 2005

"I think of most things in life as either a Bob Dylan or a Beatles song."

—All Things Digital D5 conference, 2007

"I'm an optimist in the sense that I believe humans are noble and honorable, and some of them are really smart. I have a very optimistic view of individuals. As individuals, people are inherently good. I have a somewhat more pessimistic view of people in groups."

—*Wired*, 1996

"That was one of the things that came out most clearly from this whole experience. I realized that I love my life. I really do. I've got the greatest family in the world, and I've got my work. And that's pretty much all I do. I don't socialize much or go to conferences. I love my family, and I love running Apple, and I love Pixar. And I get to do that. I'm very lucky."

—On living with cancer, *BusinessWeek*, 2004

"You can't connect the dots looking forward; you can only connect them looking backwards. So you have to trust that the dots will somehow connect in your future. You have to trust in something—your gut, destiny, life, karma, whatever. This approach has never let me down, and it has made all the difference in my life."

—Stanford University commencement address, 2005

"Much of what I stumbled into, by following my curiosity and intuition, turned out to be priceless later on."

"Equal opportunity to me more than anything means a great education."

"I don't think much about my time of life. I just get up in the morning and it's a new day."

"Think about yesterday, dream about tomorrow, but live today."

"I'm sorry, it's true. Having children really changes your view on these things. We're born, we live for a brief instant, and we die. It's been happening for a long time. Technology is not changing it much—if at all."

—*Wired*, 1996

"I didn't see it then, but it turned out that getting fired from Apple was the best thing that could have ever happened to me. The heaviness of being successful was replaced by the lightness of being a beginner again, less sure about everything. It freed me to enter one of the most creative periods of my life."

—Stanford University commencement address, 2005

"I think one of the most precious resources we all have these days is free time."

—*ABC News*, 2005

"I'll always stay connected with Apple."

—*Playboy*, 1985

"Bottom line is, I didn't return to Apple to make a fortune. I've been very lucky in my life and already have one. When I was 25, my net worth was $100 million or so. I decided then that I wasn't going to let it ruin my life. There's no way you could ever spend it all, and I don't view wealth as something that validates my intelligence."

"You know, my main reaction to this money thing is that it's humorous, all the attention to it, because it's hardly the most insightful or valuable thing that's happened to me."

—*Playboy*, 1985

"I remain extremely concerned when I see what's happening in our country, which is in many ways the luckiest place in the world. We don't seem to be excited about making our country a better place for our kids."

—*Wired*, 1996

"My self-identity does not revolve around being a businessman, though I recognize that is what I do. I think of myself more as a person who builds neat things. I like building neat things. I like making tools that are useful to people."

—*Esquire*, 1986

"I feel like somebody just punched me in the stomach and knocked all my wind out. I'm only 30 years old and I want to have a chance to continue creating things. I know I've got at least one more great computer in me. And Apple is not going to give me a chance to do that."

—*Playboy*, 1987

"I have always said if there ever came a day when I could no longer meet my duties and expectations as Apple's CEO, I would be the first to let you know. Unfortunately, that day has come."

—Memo to Apple employees, 2011

"No one wants to die. Even people who want to go to heaven don't want to die to get there. And yet death is the destination we all share. No one has ever escaped it. And that is as it should be, because Death is very likely the single best invention of Life."

—Stanford University commencement address, 2005

"And one more thing…"

—A phrase often used to unveil products towards the end of Apple presentations

"Remember the *Whole Earth Catalog*? The last edition had a photo on the back cover of a remote country road you might find yourself on while hitchhiking up to Oregon. It was a beautiful shot, and it had a caption that really grabbed me. It said: 'Stay hungry. Stay foolish.' It wasn't an ad for anything—just one of Stewart Brand's profound statements. It's wisdom. 'Stay hungry. Stay foolish.'"

—*Fortune*, 1998

"I did everything in the early days—documentation, sales, supply chain, sweeping the floors, buying chips, you name it. I put computers together with my own two hands. And as the industry grew up, I kept on doing it."

—*BusinessWeek*, 2004